I Don't Get Tech

(So, What is a Teacher to Do?)

Susan Swift

The anecdotal evidence contained in this text is rendered from my experience with the Dubuque Community School District. Like any large institution, DCSD is subject to the limitations of its structure. Some of those limitations are discussed in this book, but are not intended, in any way, to cast doubt on the overall effectiveness Dubuque Schools has on its students. My own children attended DCSD, and I have recommended this educational system to many of my friends as well as other professionals.

Contributors' essays and quotes included are used verbatim with minor editing.

In memory of
Elaine and Ray Swift

CONTENTS

Acknowledgements

For Whom the Book Tells

Prologue

1	I'm Behind	1
2	Dive In	7
3	iDumb	19
4	Let Go and Let the Tech God	27
5	An Indigo Bunting Sighting	35
6	Buzz Kill	45
7	What Tools to Use	51
8	The Flipped Classroom	61
9	Tech-tonic Shifts	69
10	Get Tech	89

ACKNOWLEDGMENTS

This book would not have been possible without the support of my friends and colleagues.

For your editing advice, thank you, James Brimeyer. For your thoughtful essays, thank you to: Dr. John Ross, Joel Miller, Deb Henkes, Sarah Blosch, Brenda Foust, Linda Jegerlehner, and Peggy Dolson. For your artistic photograph, thank you, Tyler Till.

I also give special thanks to my beloved colleagues who have either been my comrades in the tech battle or who have served as inspiration in the writing of this book: Boyd Card, Coby Culbertson, Mary Ebeling, Chad Harwick, Sandy Hoerner, Michelle Hunt, Adam Miller, David Moeller, Steph Monahan, Dee O'Brien, Kim Swift, Kristine Swift, Pilar Swift, and Karla Weber.

My heart is full of gratitude for all of you.

For Whom the Book Tells

If you are a tech-savvy teacher, put this book down now. You don't need it. (In fact, if you *are* adept at tech, you need to write your own book and let the rest of us read it.) This book is neither profound nor serious; it is, rather, practical and ordinary. Sometimes it is humorous because, well, if we don't poke fun at our foibles, then what is the point of existence? The theory embedded in each chapter is short and simple—much like the woman who conceptualized it. This book is intended for the tech-dreaded, for those teachers who feel lost, left behind, or otherwise bewildered about the technological terrain. I wrote this book for you—to give you a little hope, a few ideas, and a lot of encouragement. Believe me, if I can grasp and infuse some tech into my lesson plans, *anyone* can. We are not, after all, perfectionists, but people—teachers doing the best we can for our students. In terms of classroom technology, if you need a nudge, or perhaps a gigantic shove, to hop on the technology train, then this book is for you.

Prologue

It's 8:54 a.m. on a Wednesday at the beginning of summer. Sadly, I am not lounging in the sand on some exotic beach. Instead, I am supposed to be in the large assembly hall listening to the keynote speaker. But I'm not there either. The speaker for the second day at the teacher technology conference started at 8:30, but I am still sitting at home thinking about a book. This book. And what teachers and students need. Yesterday at the tech conference, my friend and colleague, Linda, said to me, "Susan, I'm surprised you haven't written a book yet. You know, if you write one page a day, every day, after 365 days, you've got long book." Look at me now, Linda. Look at *us*.

It's now 9:39, and I am sitting outside the keynote speaker's room. I actually went in once, snagged a piece of coffee cake and a half a mug of java, looked at a sea of non-engaged faces, and silently slipped away. I don't hear any laughter in there. I'm staying put in the sunlit foyer of the River Center in Dubuque, IA, in front of floor-to-ceiling windows and shining silver sculptures. (They say art mimics life. And I can see by the wild, curly hair on the aluminum musician in front of me that it's true; her hairdo looks just like mine in the morning.) Beyond the windows, I spy a father holding his daughter in his arms as his son, who is wearing a striped shirt and blue trunks, trails slightly behind them. Undoubtedly, they are on their way to the nearby water park. I want to join them. It's not a beach, but it's good enough. Instead, like a good professional, I stay put and brace myself for boredom.

Sometimes, like today, when I started writing this book, I feel as if I don't know anything. After thirty plus years of teaching, I'm still waiting—waiting to be certain I'm giving my students what they need. Applause erupts from the other room, and I am brought back to the reality of why I'm here: I don't get tech.

People pour from the large conference hall. I spy a couple of my collegial friends. They ask me if I liked the keynote speaker, and I say, "I don't know. I was writing a book." They think I'm joking until I show them this title page:

I Don't Get Tech

(So, What is a Teacher to Do?)

"Yeah," I say and then, "And I want you in it." My buddy, Boyd Card, a burly, bulk of a man eyes me skeptically. He wants me to be kidding, but he knows I'm not. He smiles underneath his grey, handlebar mustache, the likes of which only men like Boyd dare to sport. He and I go way back. We were both department chairpersons at a local high school, and when I started thinking about how much our school needed Writing Across the Curriculum (which, like most schools, is *still* greatly needed), I thought first of Boyd. At the time, he was what we used to call a "shop" teacher. You know, the hands-on industrial tech guy whose domain was placed in the "D Wing"—wicked, unintended metaphor. I knew that if I truly wanted Writing Across the Curriculum, or WAC, to work, I had to leave the lily-white pages of Novel-ville and reach toward grease-stenciled skin. Boyd grabbed my hand, became a writer, and prepared the best darn WAC video ever. Want to see Boyd and his WAC video? Check him out at: http://goo.gl/q4na6 (More later on shortened URL addresses like this one.)

Because Boyd worked at the Forum, our district administrative office, at the time, I reached out to him again, this time in the name of technology. Boyd didn't miss a beat. He talked. I typed: "During the keynote speaker, I found myself thinking about the time issue and how we can't get kids to stop doing what they're going to do, so we might as well join them. Let's tell them: 'We are going to get along if you let me feel like I'm in charge.' It's all an illusion." Random? Yes. And telling.

Time, technology, and letting go will be key tenets of this book. Its aim is threefold: 1. This book's primary purpose is to help you let go of your fear of technology and give you some ideas about getting started. To this end, we will explore a few, very useful tools to help you begin to dabble in classroom technology. Some will help your students become 21st Century learners, and some will make your life as a teacher more efficient. While both may feel intimidating—or even frightening—neither is complicated. Seriously. For most of you who have been hesitant to implement any technology other than what has been required, I invite you to think of technology, not as something fearful, but rather as something that is simply unfamiliar. Rest assured, *wherever* you are in your path to become a better teacher is perfectly acceptable.

2. We will, for lack of a better term, commiserate. According to vocabulary.com, "When you commiserate with your buddies, you're sharing your lousy feelings" ("Commiserate"). Tee

Hee! Now that's my kind of dictionary. We feel "lousy" because we don't get tech. And we know we should. But how? So many tweets, vines, sites, skypes, codes, modes, URLs (and tiny URLs), and your acronymic language—filled with PD and QR and PLC and PLN and LMS and AIW—we don't know where the H E double L to start. (Sidebar comment for those Dubuque teachers who have been around awhile: At least Madeline Hunter's professional development had a *name.* I still use what I learned from her about anticipatory set and teacher proximity among students.)

3. We will change the way we teach.

Before going on, I simply must give you a few fair warnings: 1. This book will rely upon the experts I trust most, my own esteemed colleagues. 2. This book will talk about a lot of other stuff besides the beginnings of being somewhat tech-savvy. I take full responsibility for allowing diversions to occur. 3. I love sentence fragments. Lots of them. All over the place. On every page. And I like beginning sentences with conjunctions. Yes, I know, you were told it is incorrect to write a sentence as such. Your teacher lied. Or didn't know any better.

I Don't Get Tech

(So, What is a Teacher to Do?)

"As a tech immigrant, I am far behind my students…"

-Peggy Dolson

Chapter 1

I'm Behind

As the saying goes, "I was in the right place at the right time." Some years ago, when I was the English department chairperson, I was visiting with our district coordinator about what were then the federal standards proposed in the wake of No Child Left Behind. Sifting through these and copies of other states' standards (at the time Iowa was holding out on such adoption), I concluded that the only glaring deficiency we had was in the area of technology. Having been the department chair for several years at the time, I realized that if I were to be an efficient and effective leader for our group of seventeen English teachers, we would, as a department, need to move forward.

To this end, I contacted our building tech guy, David Moeller, and asked him how we could enhance our classrooms with digital technology. At the time, the Learning Management System (LMS) push was in its infancy, so he suggested we build websites with electronic resources such as copies of assignments and links to videos and articles. We made the move. Google became our best friend.

A year later, Moeller offered a college class through our local Area Education Agency (AEA)—forgive the acronyms—and a group of us climbed aboard the computer bus toward more technological integration. He designed the lessons through the then newly designed Canvas LMS, and thereafter I utilized Canvas for the college classes I taught.

As the English department became more tech-adept, our building principal thought it would behoove the entire staff to become acquainted with technology in the classroom; thus, Moeller created a new group of professionals who would explore various tech resources and then make recommendations to the staff. As a part of this group, I began using Canvas Learning Management System (LMS) in my high school classroom as well, and I exaggerate not when I say it revolutionized the way I teach.

After a couple of years on this team at my high school, David Moeller was hired at the school district administrative office to fulfill the much-needed and long-overdue position of teacher leader in technology. In his new position, David created a 21st Century Technology District Pilot team, and over the course of three years, we further developed our own standards in digital literacy. It was a long journey with plenty of frustration, including trying to use and share classroom tablets—whose capabilities both in networking and power were limited—and spending over a year with a chosen learning management system ill-equipped to meet our district needs.

I share this story with you, dear reader, to illustrate the seemingly inevitable pitfalls and frustrations of incorporating technology into the very fabric of our everyday classroom practice. It is work. It is trying. It makes me want to beat up computers.

But, in the name of professionalism restraint, I carry on despite the obstacles because the digital platform is our students' world; thus, it is ours. Paradigms are the behemoths of the educational system, and they are darn slow to shift. But shift we must. And soon.

You have a tidbit of background on this mid-fifty-year-old educator's journey to the 21st Century, but what about the rest of the teachers? I can tell you from my colleagues that if you are not one of our district's pilot project members, you feel decidedly behind. We have had many educators even in our building inquire as to how they can join the ranks of the 21st Century parade. The answer is not an easy one. Our district is still struggling to figure out how to design professional development to catch the rest up. We have adopted Canvas Instructure as a district LMS, and I am hopeful its implementation will enable more teachers to dive into tech.

I imagine your pleas: you don't have anyone taking the initiative like our tech guy did; you don't have a district who is creating a long-term plan for technology integration; you don't have a principal who is on board with supporting innovation. You don't need it. Take your digital learning into your own hands. For example, create a small group of like-minded colleagues who are also feeling "behind," and start brainstorming changes you could make. Don't allow yourselves to dwell upon what can't happen—as legitimate as those concerns may be. Rather, focus on what *can* happen given your circumstances.

Fear not. Most districts are still trying to live up to the technology standards that are already in place. I think my colleague, Peggy Dolson, will help you see that you are not in the least bit alone in feeling behind:

> As a tech immigrant, I am far behind my students for various reasons—some are the district's problems, but most are of my own nature. I do not really like sitting in front of a computer. I can think of many, many other activities I would rather do, and therein lies most of the problem. I want my tech professional development to take place during in-service time with trained professionals, not on my own time. In reality, I know the separation from my students' skills is becoming an ever-widening gap. I am about to sign up for a graduate level course on how to use technology in the classroom. All the material is online, so we'll see how this goes. I guess it is my way of submerging myself slowly

and late even though people have been telling me to jump in for a while now.

"I miss rubber cement…With technology, there's nothing to sniff."

-Sarah Blosch

Chapter 2

Dive In

"I forced myself to dive in. I did one chapter at a time," said my friend and colleague, Sandy Hoerner, speaking about her fear in using Canvas Learning Management System (LMS) for the first time. If you knew Sandy, her initial anxiety would come as a surprise to you. She is Wonder Woman personified. Smart, fit, witty, and, save her introduction to technology, otherwise fearless. But these are paradigm-shifting situations we are faced with as we attempt to blend technology with teaching and learning. It is downright frightening.

You do not have to do so all at once, and you do not have to do so alone. But dive in, you must. And a scary ride it is because we are delving into unknown territory where anything that *can* go wrong probably *will*. An unfamiliar landscape filled with seemingly impossible obstacles stretches out before many older colleagues whose childhood experience was spent riding bikes rather than playing video games. Granted, using a smartphone and its apps helps, but it does not bring us up to snuff when it comes to teaching with technology. Likewise, however, in my experience teaching college level methods classes to students who have grown up in a technical world, they, too, are unequipped to mesh learning with technology, to use technology as a both an agent unto deeper learning and as a means to learn.

How do we manage the divide between the way we teach (which, for many, is the way in which *we* were taught) and the way we must begin to teach? First of all, we need support. Change, even welcome change, proves difficult without, as the Beatles song says, "a little help from our friends." As stated in chapter one, I was fortunate enough to have a resourceful tech coach at my school when I decided to take the leap. He was one of the people I spied when he came out of the keynote speaker's address mentioned in the preface. Our conversation went like this:

> Me: "Good morning, David. I'm writing a book. Here's the title page."
>
> He looks at me quizzically. I turn my computer so he can see my title, *I Don't Get Tech.* His eyes light up when he realizes I am just crazy enough to be serious.

Moeller: "Do you need a tech consultant? I'll be your tech consultant."

Me: "OK. Ah...we need a more interesting name for you."

Moeller: "But that's what I am."

I don't argue. Without this guy, I never would have had the guts to dive in. David Moeller taught me the most important aspect of turning to technology for better learning: don't wait to use it. Prolonging the inevitable plunge is deadly...just dive in. If you wait until you are comfortable knowing the mechanisms of whatever it is you want to use—whether it be Prezi, Twitter, Quizlet, Padlet, or a Smartboard—you will never use it. Such waiting is akin to not teaching a classic novel until you have read all of the literary criticism that exists before daring to assign it or waiting until you have enough money before getting married. Fabulous, unrealistic ideas.

I am in the middle of a swan dive right now, writing this book. I don't know all of the advice or help it will lend (if any!), but I am thrilled by the mid-air sensation of creating. Why shouldn't learning be like this? A thrilling dive into the unknown. Besides, why should you, as the teacher, know all of the tech answers when you probably have a handful of students in your class who can demonstrate skills for you and help assist others through the confusion?

My colleague, Linda, who is the inspiration for this book, has this to say about soliciting help:

This year my husband and I got smartphones. They were too smart for us, so we did what every parent does: we turned to our children for help. My daughter was happy to help us figure out what an app is, how we could get the ones we need, and how to put shortcuts on our phones. Her help, however, came with a just slightly condescending tone that prompted my husband and me to look at each other afterward and agree to never ask her for help with electronics again. And luckily for me, I don't need to; I have a roomful of students six hours a day that I can turn to for guidance on using the latest technology.

Students today have grown up with technology, so for them, using all these gadgets and computer programs is second nature. As teachers, we should set aside our fears of incorporating technology into our lessons because the students will always be able to catch on quickly, help each other to learn, and more often than not, show us how to better use the technology we are introducing.

Linda is spot on. I solicit the help of my students on a regular basis. Find out who your experts are and rely upon them. Pair the tech-savvy students with the struggling ones, and never, ever troubleshoot with students before they have maximized their workarounds: consulting with at least one of their peers, seeking the answer online, and, if all else fails, resorting to ctrl-alt-delete to restart. Teaching students to resist relying upon the teacher every time they hit a snag is another point to be taught and re-taught. We have trained our students well in being teacher-reliant instead of self-reliant, and, to be honest, breaking this pattern will be one of your most nagging challenges.

After you have decided to dive in, then, pick one thing. One. And, if your school does not already have access to online storage, such as Office 365 and its useful Classroom Notebook, I strongly urge you to begin with Gmail and Google docs. We can do a better job of preparing our kids for a greener, cleaner world by having them store their work in the cloud. With online saving, access to homework and papers suddenly becomes a non-issue. Google auto-saves, has a revision history, provides easy research, and allows readers to insert comments. It stores documents in folders and quickly uploads files from other resources such as your computer or a flash drive. Google offers other similar features as Microsoft Office with its docs and folders (like Word), presentations (like PowerPoint), spreadsheets (like Excel), snazzy surveys (like Forms), and drawings (um, I have no flippin' clue how to use this feature). Start using Google docs yourself both personally and professionally; it will help you become familiar with its applications.

Google, according to Search Engine Market Share, is the most popular search engine at over 94% global usage. It is built upon its Internet capabilities and accessibility and also has right click options superior to that of Microsoft. Right click in Google allows the writer to easily define words, access topical web results, and quickly conduct research. This may sound complicated but find out how simple it is in action. Create a document in Google, write some words in it, right click on one of the words, highlight "Define," and watch the Internet magic happen. Additionally, this small exercise will help you dive in!

And now, a little experiment with Google's right click in the slick and nifty research option. For example, I just did a right click on the word "nifty," and along the side of my screen pops up: a dictionary definition from merriam-webster.com; another from thefreedictionary.com; a stream of nifty links in pic form, such as "Nifty Comics"; a stock market index called "Nifty 50" (Who knew?); and a host of other nifty things.

The research option gives you an easy-to-use resource. Research papers can become active documents when you instruct students to include links in their work and invite peers to add commentary. All a user has to do is click on "Insert" and scroll down to "Comment," and others have the ability to give feedback. Another fabulous feature is the comments automatically identify the commentator as long as that person is logged in as a Google user as well. Think of the interactive research possibilities. Students writing papers together could include all kinds of resources, and even activities, into their work. Let's say said student is researching the origins of Angry Birds, which, back in 2011, was "a game for the hot new gadget of the day: Apple's iPhone" (Kendall, 2016). The student may include that it has over one billion downloads (Bertolucci, 2016), often referred to what Jarid Lukin coined "freemiums" (as cited in Manafy, 2009). Wait. Freemium? What an inventive word! And wow, a billion? (We are in the wrong profession. Alas.) Anyway, this student could include the Angry Birds site and invite others to play the game. They could report their experience as a link directly *into* the student's paper. The possibilities make me want to start the school year with research—words I never thought I would utter.

If your school district does not have its own mandates about accounts, choose Google as a way to connect with your kids. It's free and easy to use. At the very beginning of the school year, take your students into a lab or get them on their laptops and get them situated with a Gmail account if they do not already have one. Give your students access the directions online from a document you create to get them accustomed to getting directions from an electronic source. (More on sharing docs later—you will never have to make another paper copy for the kids again.) Now. Be firm about this next step. If the students do not already have a Google account and are creating one for the first time, insist on a consistent pattern for their username and password. For example, make the username the first initial and last name with a favorite number, such as sswift10@gmail.com. Then ask them to use their school ID# as their password. This will save you a ton of time. I can't begin to tell you how many kids I wanted to kill after the seventeenth time they claimed they couldn't get into their Gmail. (Kill? I use hyperbole here. It helps keep you awake while reading long passages of advice-laden directives.) Google docs will enable your students to electronically respond to each other's work and to create work together online.

The accessibility of your students' work, if created on online with either Microsoft Office or Google, will relieve you of many headaches—not the least of which is standing in line at the copy machine in the morning where murderous intent can easily gravitate from students to colleagues. Before the days of digital technology, I was standing in a line for the copy machine at 7 a.m. behind a string of other teachers who were likely as irritated as I was by the wait. When the fellow directly in front of me decided to print what was equivalent to a novella, I quipped that the Bonnie, the infamous copy lady with the dangerously long, sharp, purple nails, would have been happy to have printed such a large order for him. And speaking of large, the young man to whom I was speaking was a *big* guy. I had no recollection of this copy machine moment until the aforementioned gent told me about it years later. Adam, a dear friend of mine now, claimed he was intimidated by me that morning. I busted out loud laughing when he unleashed such a ridiculous comment. I am 5'1," petite woman. Adam is three times the size of me. It was the beginning of a beautiful relationship, though—so much so that I affectionately call him by his otherwise offensive nickname. It all came about one day when he wore an orange shirt, and I told him that with the help of a black marker, he would make a great jack-o-lantern. I know. Uncouth beyond belief. Happily, my beautifully rotund friend found it funny, and he has been my beloved "Punkin" ever since.

But, back to the point: going digital may temporarily increase frustration in the classroom but will eventually relieve annoyance elsewhere, like the copy machine. Not only that, but the next time a kid asks for yet *another* copy of the assignment (Seriously? Again?), you can tell him to bring it up online and print it out himself.

Using online docs as a method to impart information works beautifully, too. For example, I have stopped printing my syllabus. Students were assigned to read it online and come back the next day with any comments or questions. Why take up precious class time to go through a boring document, especially when, during the first day of school, that is *all* most teachers do? Boring. I get bored just *thinking* about my guidelines. I do, however, try to riddle my syllabus with my own unique voice, like this: Be on time. Why? Because when you come in late, it disrupts the whole class and makes me cranky.

Why dive in? If your district is like mine, it does its best to keep abreast of educational initiatives but getting everyone on board with effective professional development is a clunky, time-consuming endeavor. Take charge of your professional self. Get a handful of like-minded teachers and make some plans. Share your ideas with your principal and see if you can get some monetary support to connect with outside resources such as conferences, seminars, and educational agencies. You simply cannot wait if you want to be the best teacher for your kids *now*.

Listen, fellow teacher, yes, I am aware that you may be faced with limited technology in your building. A few years ago, at my school, a group of us created a tech team, and one of our guiding principles was to simply work with what we (and the students) *have*—and to avoid bemoaning what we don't. We refused to be mired in our limitations. We planned our own professional development and offered it to teachers on a voluntary basis. We refused to let the "I don't have time" excuse prevent our progress, and we refuted the nay-sayers' claims that technology is both unnecessary and counter-intuitive. The argument against such claims deserves its own book. Let it suffice to say, at this point, technology integration is paramount because the digital world is our students' platform—whether we like it or not. You have to start somewhere. Dive in!

Will you miss the days of yore if you do? Of course, but all change is coupled with parting and creating. Focus on the new possibilities as my colleague, Sarah Blosch, who teaches yearbook and newspaper, does here:

> I miss rubber cement. I miss the little brush attached to the lid, its snotty stretchiness, and the way it smelled— *especially* the way it smelled. Rubber cement could get you through a hectic newspaper or yearbook deadline, that's for sure. With technology, there's nothing to sniff. The sensory satisfaction of marking photos with a grease pen, working over the warm glow of a light table, or watching pictures slowly emerge in the darkroom is gone. Technology takes you out of the darkroom. On the upside, technology takes you out of the darkroom. And the dark. Technology has removed the three-day delay between taking pictures and

seeing them. Gone are the days when students spent a night taking photos, the following class period developing film, and the next class printing pictures only to find they are not worth the photo paper they were printed on. Programs like Photoshop and InDesign allow creativity and precision that was unfathomable when I began teaching. Students can design pages that are downright professional looking. They can manipulate text and photos and experiment with page layouts until they get it right, and none of it involves tediously cutting out columns of text in different widths late into the evening. The only things to touch are a keyboard and a mouse, but I am finding that the click of keys and mice can be soothing and that aerosol cans of keyboard duster smell pretty good, too.

"Technology is ubiquitous; it touches almost every part of our lives, our communities, and our homes."

-Deb Henkes

Chapter 3

iDumb

I think I am in love with Dee O'Brien and Deb Henkes. I have good reason. These two women, who work for our Area Education Agency (AEA), a state affiliate that assists in schools' professional development, never, ever let me believe I'm the moron I know I am. They are Mother-Teresa-nice. Support is so incredibly important when it comes to implementing technology. Thanks to Dee's assistance and immeasurable patience, I have managed the seemingly complex tasks of signing up for tech sessions and electronically submitting a syllabus for a college course I teach. For Deb's part, I showed her the introduction to this chapter as an invitation for her to share her wisdom. And as you will see in the next few pages, Deb Henkes employs a delightful sense of humor as she gives us advice regarding how to get over iDumbness:

> In my never-ending quest for world domination—I mean, for new ideas for technology integration ideas—I ran into a book at an actual brick and mortar bookstore (how I miss you, Borders!) called, *How Not to Act Old.* Since I am getting closer every day to verging on OLD, I thought I'd take a look to try to postpone the inevitable as long as possible. While flipping through the pages, I ran into a chapter on using technology, or more specifically—how to not "act old when using technology"! The tip that caught my eye was the advice about not acting like that "old" person who is proud of being above the technology tsunami. They proclaim they "don't do technology" like it's cute to be befuddled because your VCR has been blinking since 1990. Don't do that! Just quietly hire a fourteen-year-old boy to be your tech tutor.
>
> My takeaway from the chapter is that being a teacher is being a lifelong learner whether it's learning how to effectively integrate technology into your curriculum or how to change your teaching strategies to meet the needs of your current students.
>
> For the teachers who thought technology was going away—it's not. I know that some have said they don't want to jump on that bandwagon, and they simply want to continue doing things the way they have been doing them in

the classroom. They've been doing a good job and are successful. But technology is now ubiquitous; it touches almost every part of our lives, our communities, and our homes. In order to adequately prepare our students for 21st Century lives, we must provide them the experiences with active engagement, authentic audiences, problem solving, collaboration, communication and access to real-world experts that only technology can offer.

I know how it feels to be a novice at something. I know what it feels like to demonstrate a technology when things don't work. I know what it feels like to see a colleague or friend demo something only to have them click through the tech tool so fast I can never hope to follow it.

My advice is:

- You are not alone. Different teachers have different levels of understanding and different content and standards for their classrooms. Try a new technology first on a personal level, with family or friends. Students love it when you ask them for help. It gives them ownership and a chance to share their expertise. They are much more scornful of teachers who refuse to try to learn or say that technology doesn't matter than those who ask for help.

- Time is always, always a huge issue and barrier when trying to integrate technology or learn anything new. Try to develop a PLN (professional learning network) that gets right to the point and shares the tools, ideas, strategies, and tips that you need.

- I would suggest starting small with just one or two tech tools, based on your resources, that are easy to use and fit the needs of your students and content standards. Once you become comfortable with those tools, begin to add on as needed and where it fits.

- Don't be discouraged by "tech superstars." Everyone has strengths, and just as students learn differently, not all classrooms need to be the same. If the best tool for the job is paper and pencil—use it. Some of us remember when pencils were a new tech tool!

- Don't forget that everything is a learning experience. If the tech tool didn't work, what positive take-aways can be learned to help with next time? If it did work, how could you use it even more effectively? Every time you use a tech tool, you are building knowledge and experience about how tech works.

- Do remember to have fun and celebrate your success! Share what works with others and thank them for sharing their successes and learning with you.

- And lastly, if all else fails, just quietly hire your fourteen-year-old neighbor to be your tech tutor.

If you want a summary of what you should do to dive in, reread Deb's advice, set this book aside, and put it into action. She succinctly says it all—exactly what you need to do to get started with the right mindset.

Support is so important. As a pilot member of our school district's 21st Century skills team, I receive support not only from the likes of Deb from our AEA but also from our former building technology coach and now district technology leader, David Moeller. With his guidance, as well as the support of Coby Culbertson who leads our district IT, and Dr. John Ross, a tech consultant for the district, we have been able to move forward with a comprehensive, long-term digital literacy plan. I know. I'm lucky. Many of you are islands in the sea of technology, and hurricanes are coming from every direction. But remember, as stated earlier, you can *start* where I did: with a handful of like-minded colleagues and a positive, can-do attitude.

Tech support comes in many forms, including trying to get someone to rescue you when the dang machinery is uncooperative. Sometimes the simplest things escape me. Has this scenario ever happened to you? It's early morning, and I am psyched about the day's lesson—until the tech portion fails. I try every trick in my meager tech arsenal. The tech helper doesn't answer. The kids pour into the classroom. I'm left with nothing but a beautiful plan. If you are an inexperienced teacher and find yourself in a similar situation, this is the moment you declare, "I'm f'd" and join the attrition ranks. For the more experienced educator, you simply sigh and resort to Plan B—some lesson straight out of the Stone Age, similar to the kind of plan your traditional teacher busted out on *you* eons ago. And then later, when the tech person comes to assist you, you discover that some stupid cord wasn't plugged in and this was the source of your problem? Yeah. iDumb. iDumbfounded.

Always start with the basics: switches, cords, buttons, and plugs. And for heaven's sake, don't panic—even if you are being observed by an administrator. (Chances are the admin. sitting in the back of the room is even less tech-enlightened than you are.) If all systems seem a go and whatever is supposed to happen still doesn't, then do not try to understand why it worked during your prep period and won't do so now. Simply bail. Hit control, alt, delete; and restart that baby. Yes, I know it takes time. Yes, I know it is disappointing and frustrating. Yes, I know it worked during your test run and *should* work now. But it doesn't. Bail. Remember, restart is your friend.

If time allows, another great way to solve your tech problems is to toss your questions into the Internet. Don't wait around for your tech coach to find your classroom. Ask Google. Type in your question, and you will be surprised at how many sites are designed to answer the inane. For example, I typed in, "Hey, folks, iDumb, so can anyone tell me how to replace my iPhone glass?" and voilà! Someone on the other side of the country—who is *not* a technician or expert—had the answer. Believe it or not, I fixed my own iPhone and saved myself five hundred bucks. (No, I did not have insurance on the darn thing. Thought I did. But nope, didn't.) I was directed to a YouTube video that showed each step.

By the way, beware if you choose to delve into the recesses of your phone. The screws are miniscule. Be sure to buy the magnetic mat thingy for those teeny tiny suckers; it's called "Screwmat Magnet." (I'm not making this up!) Now, these makers enjoy my kind of humor; I mean, think of the giggles you could experience by simply saying, "Hi. I'd like a screwmat." I digress. (Digression can be a good thing. One of the problems I have with tech books is they don't digress enough. They get heavy into directions and multitudinous options of accomplishing the same task and never give the reader a break by making them crack a smile.) Back to my phone: it took me five hours the first time I took it apart, replaced the shattered glass, and put it back together. But then the camera didn't work—and I simply cannot live without my camera. I mean, think of the sunsets that would go undocumented. Well, it took another three hours to redo. Ugh. Double ugh. Anyway, the point is, I got all the help I needed by simply asking. And it can be surprisingly personal. The screwmat guy emailed me several times as I hit glitches and guided me through the labyrinthine guts of my phone.

(A little advice: if you are super clumsy, pay the money to protect your phone. Buy a solid case, and if you are a major klutz, such as myself, get a glass protector as well.)

As both Linda and Deb have formerly mentioned, often some of the best and timeliest support comes from the students themselves. Undoubtedly, my students are more technologically advanced than I am, and I rely upon their expertise on nearly a daily basis. One morning, when I could not get my monitor out of full screen mode, I called out S.O.S., and my student, Briton, pushed F11 to remedy the situation. I had no idea what F11 meant. Likewise, every time some student from a previous hour leaves a laptop screen on upside down (on purpose—just to be funny—the little twerp!) I simply yell out: Who can fix this dang thing? And some eager, willing, resourceful soul comes to the rescue.

Admittedly, iDumb. uDumb, too? It's OK. Not possessing any natural instincts when it comes to tech is no crime. Letting your fear of tech get the best of you, however, is. You must take the risk. When you do, you will, at first, experience a precipitous learning curve and feel dumber than ever. Sorry. (Forgive my honesty. I'm blunt. To a fault. So much so that it has cost me job positions I have wanted. I kid you not. That's OK, too, because, in part, the disappointment gave the energy and enthusiasm to write this book— and hopefully make you less fearful of change!) Fear not. It is only temporary. Learning curves are meant to be overcome.

"Is it worth it to sacrifice good teaching with the time it takes to incorporate technology?"

-Adam Miller

Chapter 4:
Let Go and Let the Tech God

I am in a conundrum. I have no idea how to fix this tech problem. (Said problem could be anything from what wire goes where to uploading documents.) Panic, like a feral animal, creeps into my chest. I want someone to save me. Someone smart. I call the building tech coach, and in a trill voice, ask:

Me: "How do I do this?"

Moeller, the tech consultant: "Keep trying. You will figure it out."

Me: "Ugh."

Eventually and somewhat slowly I learned how to figure tech things out on my own. Eventually and slowly I learned to encourage my kids to do the same. I'm afraid there is simply no getting around the frustration following your decision to dive in and to accept your iDumbness. But it's no excuse not to.

A dear colleague of mine, the aforementioned and affectionately-known-as Punkin, recently asked me, "Is it worth it to sacrifice good teaching with the time it takes to incorporate technology?" I paused. Adam, whose verbiage is typically imbued with humor and sarcasm, posed a serious, simple question. Even though I did not believe I was sacrificing good teaching (in actuality, I had never been so innovative), I understood his point and answered, "Yes." Here's why: the world's methods of communicating have already changed, and we must not only accept this reality but also begin to use it. Our kids' platform is digital, and unless we get onboard the tech train, it will leave without us.

Look around you. At the doctor's office, the nurse makes her notations on a laptop; at the auto center, the technician pecks upon a plastic-protected keyboard; in your own home, you make purchases from your computer. 'Tis the way of the world. And it is incumbent upon us to utilize these same skills in our classroom, as a means to learn. The exciting part of this is, once you let go and let the tech God, you will be amazed at how learning and teaching changes.

While incorporating 21st Century skills into the fabric of the classroom does take time, especially in the initial stages, sooner or later it *doesn't*. When my classroom was first equipped with tablets, my 9th graders soon got into the tech routine. After a few days of practice, these students would come into my classroom, immediately go to the computer cabinet, and log in to both their electronic word-processing system, and their Canvas Learning Management System. By the time class started, they had hit the link to an electronic document of *Romeo & Juliet*, and in another tab, they were ready to continue an electronic document hosting the outline of the plot. Allow me to reiterate these were high school freshmen, regular classes of twenty-eight freshmen.

The efficiency became even easier when my classroom was granted a cart full of laptops. Each student was assigned to a specific one, which they automatically grabbed at the beginning of class and got ready for the day's agenda by consulting the large, colorful screen hosting an electronic slide with initial directions. As our students are now issued individual laptops provided by the district, it is even easier. By next fall, all of our students will have an individual laptop. This may be a reality in your schools already, and if so, awesome. In this case, if your school has not implemented a learning management system, you may want to jump from here into chapter seven and get yourself going on a free version of Canvas LMS. Or, perhaps your school is nowhere near this point, and you are beckoning back to the "I'm behind" mantra discussed in chapter one. Don't fret. Remember, do what you can with what you have; do *something* to get yourself out of the fear associated with technology.

Allow me to point out a few benefits. First, my kids have become increasingly more independent. When they ask me how to do thus-and-so, I say, "Ask the tech God." Ha! In reality, I simply borrow my tech consultant's words: "Keep trying. You will figure it out." Their response: "Ugh." Upon further requests, I say, "Ask your partner, and if she/he doesn't know, ask someone else." I no longer jump to give assistance. You see, it is a paradigm shift for the students as well. They still instinctively seek the teacher's help instead of seeking the answer themselves, but with practice, they can change this adult-dependency behavior. I have witnessed it in action.

A second reason to take the time to incorporate 21st C skills into your classroom is it makes for quite natural cooperative and communicative learning. To accomplish a task, the students must rely upon each other. Let me pause to make a suggestion: put the students in partners for homework assignments. I know this sounds counterintuitive but hear me out. As mentioned previously, when I began to put my classroom on the technology locomotive, I had twenty-eight freshman students in each class but only twenty-one tablets. I refused to resort to my antiquated ways of handing out textbooks and assigning the questions at the end of a story simply for the sake of availability. How silly. So, I put my kids with a partner for the *Romeo and Juliet* unit. Together, they wrote the outline of the plot. Together they conducted research on a Shakespearean subject. Together, they shared the electronic link to the text.

This doesn't mean they created the same product, if you will. Rather, they supported each other in similar tasks. For example, I assigned the same Shakespearean research topic to both partners, but they had to share a tablet and work together to find different sites and different information on the same subject. Likewise, they had to find different images representing their topics to post on their learning management system page. In essence, they were forced to work together to gather, discuss, and publicize their information for the rest of the class to access. What at first seemed like a problem (not enough tablets for everyone) turned out to be a more inventive, collaborative, and "real world" manner of accomplishing a task. I have found that as I assign new homework to my students, if they don't get it, I simply ask, "Who is your partner?" and then instruct them to inquire there.

Even though now each student has a laptop, and the need to work together no longer exists, I often assign either groups or partners to projects because of what I discovered in the years when I did not have enough devices to go around: students did more quality work when assigned collaborative tasks. I was so intrigued by the nature of this phenomena that one year I set my own professional learning goal to incorporate more collective assignments and discussions into classroom practice. During second semester, I looked at the homework data from students who were either in "D" or "F" range. Their independent homework average was in the 40s while their cooperative homework was in the 70s. I redesigned almost all of the homework, including projects and discussions, so that it reflected both collaborative and independent grades. Because their scores on the collaborative were, by comparison, significantly higher, and because so many of the learning opportunities for the rest of the semester were, in part, group work, *all* of the previously failing or nearly failing students passed the class.

Creating classrooms where students are provided with opportunities to work with others helps them both navigate the tech realm with assistance and allows them to practice the much-needed skill we call, well, talking. (Note: you may have to help your students comprehend what face-to-face conversation is!)

While using technology can bring about more effective student learning and more risk-taking planning by the teacher, using technology also poses its frustrations. But then, doesn't everything? A pretty little word called patience will help. And when that reaches the end of what is humanly possible, I say, supplant outright irritation with humor. In the following scenario, I was having difficulty with PowerSchool, "a student information system that allows us to manage a wide range of information, including the following: grades, attendance, tests, demographics, activities, courses, and photos" (Schwartz, 2017). Well, that all sounds very slick, but let me tell you, PowerSchool (or whatever grading system in use at a school), like the kids, has a tendency to misbehave. Here's an example of how I managed my frustration with humor in an email to Chad, the guy who fixes computer stuff in our building:

To: charwick...

Subject: stupid PowerSchool!

Chad,

When I am feeling challenged by technology, I do what the kids do when they don't understand a book: call it stupid. It gives me a false sense of intellectual security. Anyway, to launch the Gradebook, it wants me to update Java, which, of course, I can't do because the Tech Gods have deemed me unworthy of such power. (They, too, are stupid!) Sooooo, will you help me, please, by just giving me your administrative password? I jest. Will you come by and save me from defenestrating this thing and losing my job?

Thanks, swifty

As a result, Chad came to the rescue, not physically but remotely via a thingy called VNC or virtual network computing. VNC is a "remote pc access...that can display the screen of another computer (via Internet or network) on your own screen ("Ultra VNC"). Watching your computer being controlled by someone else whom you cannot see is a bit surreal, but, hey, if it saves time, steps, and classroom interruption, all the better.

Whether it be your state's agencies, your district's leaders, your building's staff, your trusted colleagues, or your own students, support is essential. Find it and use it wherever you can get it. Gone are the lone star days of trying to troubleshoot by yourself or of thinking that in order to be an adequate teacher, you need to know all of the tech answers. You can't. It moves too fast and shifts too frequently. Let Go and Let the Tech God!

So many lenses; so little time.

Chapter 5

An Indigo Bunting Sighting
Only Needs One Pair of Binoculars

An indigo bunting—have you ever seen one? Imagine you are walking along a bygone railroad track, one that used to bear the weight of rumbling trains but now serves as a lovely wooded path. To your right, rocks rise like monoliths from a forgotten time, and to your left, a stream rushes over rocks. A meadow unfolds before you, and from its edge, a flash of electric blue flits upon the backdrop of green leaves. You stand still, raise your binoculars, and set your sights on the surprising delight of an indigo bunting.

(The pic above is thanks to Google docs: right click, select "research," and, boom, indigo bunting. Use your imagination to see the beautiful blue.) I right clicked on "page source" to try to cite this source and was startled by about three thousand miles of computer code. Then I clicked on "usage rights" and found this:

- Free to use or share
- Your results will only include content that is either labeled as public domain or carry a license that allows you to copy or redistribute its content

Who knew?

Large school districts, bless them, do their best to ensure teachers are receiving the professional development (PD) they need to meet the standards of the feds as well as those set by their respective states. The problem is, they so often do it poorly—not because they are nincompoops, but because, within the current paradigm for PD, they are up against an impossible task. In an effort to get the weaker teachers to be less so, they only succeed in marginalizing those of us who are mediocre. And the gifted teachers, such as my esteemed colleague, Steph Monahan (who utilizes technology in her classroom more than anyone else I know) have no choice but to become outright enraged. As they should. When was the last time you participated in professional development that was worth setting aside all of your own particular professional goals? I rest my case.

Back to the binocular metaphor. Our district has several initiatives happening at once. Each of these has common features, and each is an effective lens in its own right. The problem is we don't know where to look. I have one pair of binoculars on the trail. I zero in. I see the bird. I don't carry several pairs in my pocket because to switch from one set to the other would take me away from what is important: seeing the bird. So it is with professional development. I do not need several instruments to accomplish the same task; I need one good one. Otherwise, rather than using a single, effective lens, I am spending too much of my time fine tuning the various tools and not enough time looking at what is important: seeing the student.

At a recent in-service day, we were asked to take a student task and examine how and where it meets the state standards. The curriculum director was new and gave us no lens with which to complete this task. A previous encounter with her impervious attitude helped me resist challenging her for further clarification on exactly *how* this task should be accomplished. In the last few years, we have been utilizing a veritable buffet of lenses in which to view these standards, known as the Iowa Core Curriculum (ICC), including: Jan Chappuis's *Seven Strategies on Assessment for Learning* (2010), also called AFL; Authentic Intellectual Work (AIW) from the Center of Intellectual Work (out of UW-Madison, my beloved alma mater); and our district's 21st Century skills chart, called "The Continuum," which is modeled after the International Standards for Technology Education (ISTE). In addition, we have, of late, influences from Wiggins and McTighe's *Understanding by Design* (2005), as well as Jim Burke's *What's the Big Idea?: Question-Driven Units to Motivate Reading, Writing, and Thinking* (2010), along with the district's emphasis on "I can" statements and the state's movement toward standards-based grading. It's dizzying! (And these standout influences do not even include my own professional gurus, such as Kelly Gallagher, Penny Kittle, Anne Lamott, and Billy Collins.) So many lenses; so little time. It begs the question: Where does an educator specifically look?

With my multitudinous monocles, I get ready to plunge into my AP Lit class's first assignment, a group essay assignment over the novel *1984*. This is what I came up with that morning as I looked through the district's many lenses:

Lens #1: Backwards Design

From *Understanding by Design* (Wiggins and McTighe), I landed upon what would result in the students' end product: final draft of a collaborative essay. I place this first...if you don't know why, you may want to read their book. It's worth it. (Still can't believe Wiggins has passed.)

Lens #2: Big Ideas & Essential Questions

From Burke's ideas, I formulated the following comments and questions: 1. Authors craft their writing to invite specific reactions in readers. What tools does the author employ to manipulate the reader's reaction to text? 2. Authors use a variety of literary elements such as symbol, motif, allusion, and metaphor to create a universal message. What is the underlying, implicit, more universal message in the text?

Lens #3: Iowa Core Curriculum (ICC)

From the Iowa Core Curriculum, I selected the following core standards to guide the learning:

Production and Distribution of Writing

W.11-12.4. Produce clear and coherent writing in which the development, organization, and style are appropriate to task, purpose, and audience.

W.11-12.5. Develop and strengthen writing as needed by planning, revising, editing, rewriting, or trying a new approach, focusing on addressing what is most significant for a specific purpose and audience.

W.11-12.6. Use technology, including the Internet, to produce, publish, and update individual or shared writing products in response to ongoing feedback, including new arguments or information.

Research to Build and Present Knowledge

W.11-12.9. Draw evidence from literary or informational texts to support analysis, reflection, and research.

Lens #4: Seven Strategies & Learning Targets

From *Seven Strategies of Assessment for Learning*, I followed Chappuis's direction and determined the following:

Learning Target: to write an AP essay that demonstrates understanding of author's craft and purpose and the effects the writer's craft has on the reader

Knowledge needed: The student will identify literary devices in the text.

Reasoning: The student will make inferences, identify the writer's style, and examine the effects of the literary devices.

Skills: The student will deconstruct text, collaborate on writing, work in small response groups, accept and give constructive criticism, and effectively assess using an evidence-based rubric (EBR).

Product: The student will engage in supportive discussions lending effective feedback, produce EBR rubrics for peer and self, and utilize a writing process to produce a final draft of an essay.

Lens #5: 21st C skills

Our school district's plan to implement 21st Century skills utilizes the verbiage from the International Society for Technology in Education (ISTE) Standard 1, stating that students will "demonstrate creative thinking, construct knowledge, and develop innovative products and processes using technology." To this end, students will create a shared Google doc to create brainstorming notes, develop an action plan for writing the essay, and collaborate to write the essay. The final draft of the essay will be submitted to Canvas LMS. Students will also, as the ISTE Standard 2 states, "use digital media and environments to communicate and work collaboratively, including at a distance, to support individual learning and contribute to the learning of others." (Speaking of teaching with technology, a visit to the ISTE website would also be well worth your while.)

Lens #6: Assessment for Learning Tool

Students will use an evidence-based rubric, I created in conjunction with the College Board standards, to assess their progress on the essay. The same EBR will be used for the summative assessment.

Impressive? Hmmm…impressively redundant. I showed this to my AIW/PLC/21stC Pioneer group. (Confused by my acronymic grouping? Me, too.) Anyway, when I showed this to three of my colleagues, their only concern was that I *not* show it to anyone else lest we be required to do such lengthy "proof" in all we do. It's a legitimate concern. In an effort to make us better educators, administrators often seek the most current and sound educational initiatives—unfortunately and typically, a myriad of them. When they introduce them to the rest of us, they toss out the term "research-based" and expect us to jump up and down with newfound religious fervor. Inevitably, they claim that *this* initiative will *not* be a fly-by-night production, but rather, a staid and permanent fixture in our pedagogy. At such junctures, those of us in the trenches listen attentively and heave a collective sigh.

I have two pieces of advice to educational theorists: 1. Stop trying to be a brighter "Bloom." The reconfiguring of Bloom's taxonomy says nothing new. He said it well the first time. Leave it alone. It's not that complicated. We do not need multitudinous charts, graphs, wheels, methods, and modes to comprehend simple ideas. It takes but a couple probing questions to bring your classroom to the brink of critical thinking. The complexity of it all should manifest in the student work, not in that which defines it.

And 2. Stop insisting upon sameness. I used to be our English department chairperson; it was one of the few endeavors I did very well. After over a decade, I gave it up. I could no longer take the inane. The edicts at the hands of a new registrar who insisted upon sameness dismantled years of effective change we made in our curriculum and did away with the cross-curricular class growth we were experiencing. It's a shame what we do to decent educators in the wake of sameness.

Sameness affects us as teachers by way of professional development as well. Your district may make claim to differentiated learning, but it only applies to what you do with your students in the classroom. It clearly does not apply to how they deliver professional development. Most wholesale PD depends upon sameness rather than differentiation. We spend countless hours figuring out how we are going to accomplish the same standards in the same way with the same materials. What a waste. Alas, 'tis fodder for another book. Plus, such thoughts make me wax grim—and while it is true that one of the goals of this text is to "commiserate," my primary aim to encourage.

Thus, let's move on to positive thoughts unto how we can effectively create change, despite our institutional limitations. Let us examine an effective way to incorporate 21st Century skills into professional development. For the first time in my history with our district, we are delivering PD where it matters most: in the classroom, close to the bone. I offer this as a model for those of you who are in leadership roles and those of you who could be instrumental in implementing 21st C skills ideas for your department/school/district. First, we have a district leader in technology (aka my tech consultant) who is a former teacher; this is key. He thinks like a teacher because he is one. His focus is student learning. Each building has a technology coach who is active in the development of 21st C skills inside the classroom; this person serves as a resource as well as a hands-on assistant.

We have a pilot tech team of teachers who are investigating new technologies as an avenue for more effective learning. I am a part of this twenty-two-person team. Within our building, the teachers on this initial pilot team participated with three days of large group district meetings in addition to three PD days of our own design. Also, we met with consultants, the district leader in technology, the building tech coach, and other educators a couple of times a year to share our professional goals and brainstorm effective ways to meet them. Our framework is the aforementioned "Continuum." (The wordsmith in me likes its being a word instead of an acronym.) The four areas of the Continuum are: the informed learner, the creative learner, the cooperative learner, and the critical learner. (Lovely titles. I like them and understand them as larger concepts. Never underestimate the power of words. Language is as important as a lens as it is in literature.)

We also work with outside observers who use the Continuum as a means to score what is happening in the classroom. I use the word "score" for lack of a better word and because it does boil down to a single number. What's different about this score as opposed to the typical way we think of the word is that it does not wield judgment. It simply observes. Thereafter, individual teachers meet with the tech coach to discuss how the teacher viewed the class period in light of the lesson plan goal, how the observers' scores inform the teacher, and to what extent the score supports the teacher and/or encourages change.

This professional development is different—not because it is rubric-free but because it is rubric-friendly. The rubric is given only its due as an imperfect tool we use to guide what we do. As a teacher, I am not criticized. I am supported. The very basis of the PD is ingrained in conversation and reflection as a means to ignite more meaningful, critical learning. Because the observed teacher guides the conversation, it works.

"They were in the classroom at one time, but they aren't anymore, and that makes all the difference."

-Michelle Hunt

Chapter 6

Buzz Kill

Tech presenter at conference: "I have many tools in my box: I use this, I use this, I use this, I use this, I use this, I use this, I use this, I use this." Tech presenter takes brief breath.

Bewildered audience sighs.

Tech presenter: "And I use this!"

Bewildered audience plays "Words with Friends" on new district-purchased iPad.

If we were reading the *Game of Thrones* series now, we would call this style of presenting, as R.R. Martin puts it, a "Storm of Swords." In theory, it is helpful to pull out myriad "tools" from the "box," but, in reality, it confounds. As my friend Michelle so eloquently states, "The presentation becomes about them and not about us. It needs to be about your audience."

Toolbox falls in the stupid buzzword category as do "ratchet it up," "roll out," and "share out." Share out? Why not, simply, share? This point brings out the picky English teacher in me. The cranky one. In district meetings, when we are asked to "Read and share out...," I literally have to bite my tongue to prevent myself from shouting, "Do you mean to use the word 'out' as an adverb or a preposition in this annoying instance?" Dispense with the buzz. Give me your unique way of saying what you mean.

After sharing my tech presenter experiences with my sister, Kristi, a grade school teacher, she says exactly what she means:

> Why don't we leave when there is a bad presenter? If everyone left, it would very quickly eliminate the bad ones. We leave a bad play, a bad concert, a bad movie. Why don't we leave a bad presenter? And by not leaving, we are propagating bad presenters. Power. We don't know when to use our power and when not to. A little bit of power makes some people [colorful expletive] horrible. You need to write a book about power next, Suz.

Hmmm...Maybe I will include power in this one. After all, powerful people coin buzzwords in an effort to establish a common language. I have an idea: Let's build an uncommon one. I don't want to hate words—especially ones I am fond of. Case in point: I used to like the word "authentic." It was rarely used because, well, so few things truly *are* authentic. Then came AIW: authentic intellectual work. We have beaten the word authentic and its sidekick acronym to smithereens. Suddenly I'm so sick of the term that I no longer have the desire to be my authentic self.

Whether it be a supposed expert flown in as a keynote speaker or an administrator from your district's office, part of the problem with presenters is, as my dear friend Michelle Hunt puts it: "They were in the classroom at one time, but they aren't anymore, and that makes all the difference." Indeed.

This is why a presenter such as Kelly Gallagher inspires. He does not dump an unfamiliar and overloaded toolbox upon his audience. He tells stories. Real ones. *Authentic* ones about the classroom in which he continues to teach. He encourages his audience by way of words, of language, of anecdotes with very human, imperfect outcomes.

Let's be real, shall we? Authentic, as it were? Too little time is spent honing in on what students need and how teachers can help them attain what they need. We do not need a binder full of reading strategy examples nobody will ever consult. We need conversation. We cannot afford to spend copious amounts of time combing through the state's curriculum and playing jigsaw with our lessons to ensure we are meeting standards. That is someone else's job.

We need time. We need time to figure things out for ourselves. District folk: you come up with select focus questions and then leave us alone to answer them. Allow me to pose a few in keeping with our current initiatives: How can students be more involved in using and creating formative assessments? How can students engage in critical thinking during the course of a unit? How can students produce work that is more meaningful to them? How can students work with their communities and help define and understand our world? Give us the resources, the books, the sites, the what-have-you, and then leave us alone to manage our particular work in addressing these questions.

When a former leader in my district wanted to get to a point in a project with urgency, she would use the term "quick and dirty." We just need a "quick and dirty" go at this. Really? I suppose she meant the phrase as opposed to time-consuming and clear, but it sounded more like a perversity. Each time she uttered it, I wanted to play the petulant child and toss out a return buzzword phrase: "What would that look like?"

What's the buzz about? It is currently some kind of frenetic dance of the bumblebee. (I can hear Rimsky-Korsakov's "Flight of the Bumblebee" ringing in my ears right now.) I want to tell them to stop buzzing around and land upon the flower already. Settle down. Explain what you want in the simplest, fewest words, like this: 1. student-centered classroom, 2. project-based work, 3. formative assessments, 4. 21st C skills, and 5. real world application and engagement. Worthy endeavors are these. Stop making them complicated by couching them in "rich" buzz lingo and flinging strategies every which way.

Here's a word rendered practically negligible in the wake of nauseating buzzwords: fun. Teachers who are there for the paycheck (meagre as it may be) denounce the word because they understand one key component of it: work. Yes, for a lesson to be fun, it takes time, energy, creativity, and craft. The result, however, is increased student engagement. If a teacher incorporates fun, then half the battle is already won as the students are not only there but also present. Consider the following transaction between my sister and her grandson:

It broke my heart when Tristan told me in April, "Yeah, Gramma Kristine, I don't like learning. I like art and music and gym." Tristan is not overly talented in art and music, so, what are these disciplines presenting that the others are not? Subsequently, I didn't buy a bunch of books and flashcards. I got online and looked up games for teaching reading. Tristan came in and sat down and loved it. I told him, "See, you like learning; it's just that your teachers didn't make it fun."

Our students already associate technology usage with fun because so much of their pastimes utilize it. Whether it be gaming, connecting on social media, creating a Snapchat, or searching YouTube, kids are tuned in. We must look past the interruptive potential of the cell phone in class and begin to generate new methods to explore, express, and reveal learning.

Lovely. But, how? Read on...

I make no apologies for being a huge Google fan.

Chapter 7

What Tools to Use

As promised at the beginning of the book, I will share a few tech tools I use every day. The following are extremely useful and effective in my everyday classroom practice: an opening agenda screen, powered by either Google Slides or PowerPoint; Canvas Learning Management System (LMS), which has a free version available to you; Symbaloo, "a visual bookmarking tool" ("Why Use Symbaloo?"); Pandora, which plays online music stations; Diigo, a place to organize professional groups and share professional articles; Ginger, a virtual editing program; and Google—used for both professional and personal purposes.

Canvas Learning Management System (LMS)

If your district isn't already considering a learning management system, also known as an LMS, it likely soon will be. This is the inevitable (and if chosen well and used wisely, the *welcome*) wave of the future. As we move away from paper and pen and lean toward a green delivery and acquisition of information, an LMS provides the means to access content, take tests and quizzes, analyze data, share documents, and, perhaps most importantly, provide student collaboration. I advise you not to wait for your district to wrap its mind around the way in which it will choose and use an LMS. Rather, choose the free version of the LMS called Canvas. This system is user-friendly as well as aesthetically pleasing.

I cannot say enough about this product; I have used it for years both as the free version and as our district's adopted LMS program. User-friendly, slick, supportive, and innovative, Canvas offers it all. Soon gone are the days of worksheets and textbooks. Accept it. I say, good riddance. Our students' spines have suffered under the burden of heavily laden textbooks. Likewise, their access to content has been at the mercy of the teacher's own hard copies of assignments laboriously printed at the copy machine; before long, it will be archaic. Why not hop on the tech bandwagon now? It isn't a fad; it's a shift. It isn't a phenomenon; it's a reality. Plus, Canvas has a free teacher account that is easy to use and will *eventually* save you copious amounts of time and energy. Furthermore, it will help your students become more responsible for and independent in their own learning. It supplies myriad tutorials and an extremely beneficial person-to-person help desk to assist you—yes, even with the free account.

An aside: when our district was considering which LMS to use, we narrowed it down to three: Brainhoney, Blackboard, and Canvas. Initially, we went with Brainhoney because it was the only company that guaranteed seamless integration with our grading system, PowerSchool. To make a long (that is an entire yearlong) story short, its promises proved false. In addition, Brainhoney was clunky to use. I was thrilled when we abandoned our first choice and went with a superior and familiar one, Canvas.

Other Good Classroom Stuff

If you choose to use a learning management system, you and your students will be exposed to all sorts of online options, such as quizzes, discussion boards, assignment submissions, rubrics, feedback, files, announcements, collaborations, videos, and more. You will also have access to a "Commons" where other teachers have shared their own useful materials and made them available for others to replicate. One of the major benefits of using an LMS is its host of readily accessible in-house features.

If you do not choose to use an LMS, however, I have a few other resources you may want to explore. These include: **Kahoot**, an online quiz maker/taker; **Poll Everywhere**, an interactive polling service; **Prezi**, an electronic presentation site; **SurveyMonkey**, for creating, you guessed it, surveys; and **Padlet,** an electronic, collaborative bulletin board. You may furthermore consider building your own teacher website which could give you and your students electronic access to links, assignments, blogs, etc. If your school has invested in and uses O365, you may want to consider using **OneNote Classroom** as a method of digitally featuring and organizing your class.

LastPass

Can you trust a single website with *all* of your passwords? Yes. You can. I did some investigative research about the validity and reliability of it before I joined. This included asking my very paranoid, tech-savvy consultant. It is my first stop in the cyberworld each morning. "Everybody should install and use a password manager. Without a password manager, you'll find yourself using simple-minded passwords like Password1, or memorizing one strong password and using it over and over" (Rubenking, 2018). And this is risky. With LastPass, you will only have to put your password in once; thereafter, never again. Furthermore, when you are signed in and go to a new site where you have created a new password, a pop-up will appear and ask if you would like LastPass to remember this new site and password. "Don't be a dupe; start using a password manager right away." (Rubenking, 2019).

Can you Symbaloo?

My cyberstop number two in the morn: Symbaloo. This is an easy-access, free site designed to house all of your most frequent websites. Log in and you are presented with fifty-two tiles awaiting your favorite web site addresses. And that's only one page. You can create a multitude of pages geared toward different subjects, such as:

research, work, travel, shopping, etc. This site also contains sharing features so you can create pages, say for a specific student task, and share it with others. It hosts countless other pages open to the public as well. I not only use this for my own professional and personal needs, but I also use it as a means to help my students keep track of their various school-related sites: PowerSchool; Canvas Learning Management System; Office 365 or Google docs; our school's library site; the state agency's various resources, including great databases; and MyAccess writing program. On the same page, I encourage them to create tiles for Purdue Owl, one of the best research resources, as well as easybib, one of the best resources for electronically producing a bibliography. Some students take initiative to create new pages for their own personal use.

Pandora: online music radio

To help create an inviting environment, I like to have music playing while students enter the classroom. For $4.99 a month, you too can enjoy advertisement-free tunes and create your own stations. (The subscription is free, with advertisements.) Once you select a station, for example, let's say I type in: *Hamilton*, then the station will play songs not only from that musical but also from similar ones in the show tune genre. Each selection features a thumbs-up and thumbs-down icon that further enables you to streamline your preferences. My stations span the gamut from Celtic Women to Slim Shady, from Krishna Das to Jason Aldean. Students get in on the action and ask for artists they enjoy, and the library keeps expanding. Special filters allow you to choose only school-appropriate numbers. (Incidentally, Pandora's phone app can prevent you from having to listen to insipid radio commercials while driving home at the end of a long school day.)

What are Add-ons, Plug-ins, and Extensions?

First of all, these three terms, while likely slightly different in their origin, are often used synonymously. No matter what the term, an add-on, plug-in, or extension is a component added to your web browser that enables certain functions on the computer when the browser is opened. Extensions and plug-ins are additional features that did not automatically come with your browser, thus the term: add-on. Most extensions are free and easily downloaded with a few short steps. The most useful extensions I use for classroom purposes are Ginger and Diigo. Ginger is a free extension that auto-corrects your grammar and punctuation. (Yes, even an English major should use such a product.) Diigo is an awesome add-on that allows you to earmark web addresses of articles, comment upon them, and form groups of other people who may be interested in the same topic. It is a fantastic means by which to build—and share—professional articles. I use Diigo both with my professional learning community and with colleagues who take my college classes.

On a personal level, plug-ins are useful as well. For example, I downloaded the add-on entitled PriceBlink, so when I am on the Internet cruising through online sites to shop, PriceBlink lets me know if I can find the same product elsewhere online for a cheaper price.

URL shorteners

As you delve into the throes of technology, you will find yourself in Link-land and in need of shorter URL addresses. Google (again!) can shorten these for you at goo.gl. But if you are wanting a more specialized address with specific, and identifiable titles, use tinyURL.com. There you can create both random, shorter links and customized ones.

Google

I make no apologies for being a huge Google fan. Google's Gmail, docs, search, research, scholar, images, and calendar have made my teaching and personal life more pleasant. Google makes everything easier. Even though I now require my students to use Microsoft Office (O365) as advised by my school district (because of access rights and age-appropriate networking), Google is far ahead in its educational features and simplicity. While O365 has improved with fewer glitches, overall, it still has issues with seamless uploading from the desktop version to the cloud. I cannot begin to tell you how many times I have lost my daily PowerPoint slide's updates—so many that I returned to using Google slides simply to relieve myself of the recurring frustration. And I can't for the life of me understand why the O365 online version does not employ all of the features the desktop does. Furthermore, (and this will be the end of my rant) as a teacher who spends most of her time reading and responding to essays, I like Google's optional feature allowing editing privileges to others. While I have not used **Google Classroom**, it functions as another tool for easy sharing of electronic documents between teachers and students. My daughter, Mary, uses it in her grade school classroom, and she states, "It can also connect to a host of online curricula and websites that are Google Classroom compatible, making it easier to upload assignments. It offers a seamless integration, for example, with my Pearson Realized pilot program."

Electronic Slides

Each day my students enter the classroom with what Madeline Hunter termed an "anticipatory set." I call it the means to never have to answer the indomitable question: What are we doing today? My slide includes: the class, the date, the homework, the agenda for the day, and any pertinent announcements and links. It's big. It's bold. It's brilliant. From senior AP literature students to my regular English ninth graders, all consult the screen upon their entrance to the room. I usually include a visual, symbolic accompaniment to help catch their attention. Entertainingly colorful and basically informative, the daily slide is the beginning of their classroom engagement. They know what *to* expect, and they know what will be expected *of* them. The slide is also accessible online at the LMS, so if students are absent, they can still stay connected with what had happened that day in the classroom. (Yes, I know this potential probably only exists in the La La Land segment of my brain.)

Projectors

If your school has installed a full screen projector into your classroom, I suggest you use it. If your school has not installed such a gem, I propose you ask them to do so. (And if you can get them to provide you with a Smartboard, all the better.) Here is how I landed a projector in my classroom. I call this story, Beware the Pronouns or Existentialist Theory at Work:

District installer guy enters my classroom.

He says: "They want a wireless projector in every classroom."

Me: "Who are 'they'?"

Installer guy: "The assistant superintendent." (ardent supporter of classroom technology)

Me: "Enough said."

The next day, Chad, our school's resident break/fix dude, comes in to make certain my new projector is working.

Chad: "They said everyone wants a wireless projector."

Me: "Who are 'they'?" (Déjà vu ensues here.)

Chad: "Coby" (effective district IT director)

Me: "Who is everyone?"

Chad: "I don't know."

Me: "Does Coby know?"

Chad: "I don't know."

Ah, such is life in the trenches. Usually it's warfare, but on occasion, magic sweeps in and makes everything temporarily delicious. I got a sweet projector without even asking.

If you have a projector, I encourage you to make use of it with a daily agenda slide from either PowerPoint or Google Slides—ahem, you already know my preference.

"As educators, we are privileged to be a part of the current revolution in education."

-Brenda Foust

Chapter 8
The Flipped Classroom

Once you begin to use technology as a common practice in your classroom, you will find yourself inventing new teaching modalities. What used to be introduced as direct instruction during class, for example, may morph into a video you record and have your students view on their own time. In other words, we begin to "flip" where, when, and even how we teach. With the increase in accessibility of the Internet via hotspots as well as the movement toward schools providing computers for every student, the learning options grow. For example, what was once considered a Midwestern snow day could transform into a teaching opportunity. (Wait. What? No. Instead, bring on the toboggans!)

Brenda Foust, a secondary history teacher and tech devotee, offers these encouraging words:

As educators, we are privileged to be a part of the current revolution in education. We are moving from the Industrial Age to the Technological Revolution of the 21st Century. Whether you are just acquiring technological tools like a tablet, iPad or laptop or are a one-to-one school, the use of technology in the classroom is having a greater impact on students than any other moment in history. For the first time ever, students can have their teachers with them in the privacy of their home at night and on weekends. This is accomplished through learning management systems, flipped lessons, Skype, LinkedIn, Google Chat and a myriad assortment of other tools. For the first time, teachers are maximizing classroom time by teaching the low level Blooms, or level 1 or 2 Depth of Knowledge Chart, at home. This allows teachers to infuse classroom time with authentic tasks that include high level thinking and real-world problem solving with the goal of impacting an audience beyond school. Our students are so lucky. Never before have we as humans had this great capacity for learning. It is our responsibility as educators to actively pursue new training in this field to meet the needs of our learners. Our students are growing in up in the digital age, and, as educators, we have a responsibility to meet their new and ever-changing needs. No matter how long you have been in the classroom, there is a contribution piece for you. Get on board—be a part of the excitement! This is going to be an adventure! Like the explorers of centuries ago, we are charting new territory. Let's do it together!

Joel Miller, also a high school social studies teacher, has further advice on the establishing the flipped classroom in his following essay.

To Flip Without the Flop
Joel Miller

The first obstacle in flipping the classroom is to clearly define what the phrase means. Even to administration and some experts, this seems to cause confusion based on faulty assumptions. Does flipping the classroom refer to tech integration into the daily classroom, or does it refer to using technology to facilitate an alternative classroom meeting schedule? While some of the methods and activities a teacher could use would work for both, there are instructional plans that may be exclusive to one purpose or the other. Before endeavoring to flip the classroom, the teacher must define its purpose and have all the stakeholders on board.

I am not an expert on this topic. I am an average teacher who just happens to have experience in this area. I have taught five semesters at the college level in a hybrid/blended format (meet once face-to-face weekly and once online per week) and two semesters at the high school level in a hybrid/blended format (meet three days face-to-face and two days online per week). From my experience, high school students and college students are more similar than different, and the same challenges and successes exist at both levels. Even more importantly, I am not a cutting-edge technology integrator. Rather, I am apprehensive and cautious about tech integration. That said, technology has allowed me to do some things that I would not have been able to do in the classroom without it, and it has allowed me to do some things better than I would have been able to do with more traditional methods. In short, it is a tool a teacher can selectively use to become much more effective.

Probably the most important consideration when flipping the classroom is to envision what the learner will be doing outside of the classroom. Even if you are doing a hybrid schedule where a student has an entire period to complete online tasks, it is a mistake to think that a learner will be sitting in front of an electronic device for an extended and continuous period of time. Learners will not be a captive audience like they are when they are sitting in your actual physical classroom. The teacher has to respect the students' time and create meaningful and easily completed tasks. If students get confused right away, they will simply give up, and the learning opportunity will be wasted. To minimize this, I recommend introducing, modeling, and demonstrating what the students will be doing online before you see them again face-to-face. It often takes as much time to explain the online task as it will take for the students to complete the online task. You must be prepared to invest face-to-face time in order to facilitate the online learning activity later. Be careful not create an online learning activity that the learner would not like completing in a face-to-face environment. They have to want to do the learning activity. Of course, the same factors exist as would for other homework guidelines. Make sure that they have enough time to complete the task (due to their schedules away from school), and vary the types of activities you assign.

The biggest thing that surprised me was the myth of saving time by flipping the classroom. It does not save as much time as you would think. I did not realize how much time I would have to spend as we met face-to-face explaining what would happen online. When we are teaching face-to-face, much of this is viewed as guided practice. However, online, one does not necessarily have all of the luxuries a physical presence would offer. Because verbal directions can readily be forgotten, written directions for the students' online activities have to be more concrete, detailed, and precise. Moreover, the teacher must establish clear communication procedures with the students when they are online. Monitoring this takes time too, especially as the frequency of "check-ins" occur. This becomes even more pronounced with online discussions. The instructor must be present and monitor the online communication and learning. It is an acquired skill to not dominate the discussion, but keep it moving forward. Students, too, must be trained on online learning etiquette and procedures. This also takes time, especially before this type of learning becomes common school-wide.

From my experience at both the high school and college level, I would caution against a true flip (at least until the culture changes and the learners walk into your classroom with years of experience with this type of learning and the expectations that go along with it). A true flip is where they learn the material as homework, and they interact with it the next day in a face-to-face environment. As I implied earlier, most of my experience is with students who have not had much contact with the whole flipped online environment. Thus, I have been forced at both levels to not make the online learning activities as crucial, but rather, merely supplemental or enriching. Because the teacher is accountable for student learning, you must be prepared if only a minority of students completes the online tasks. I would advise against designing the next face-to-face learning activity predicated on the completion of the previous online learning activity. This could lead to your frustration and potentially giving up on this whole approach. I sought the advice of an administrator on this dilemma and was told to make them accountable grade-wise for what they were doing or not doing online. I would recommend against this as it could create many more problems than it solves. I would merely recommend making it a minor part of their grade (at least until the students are used to this type of learning before they walk into your classroom). Thus, I would, rather than providing direct online instruction, have the students perform enrichment activities, collaborate, or discuss online. While this may seem like it is limiting the impact of the flipping experience, the educator can still create a great learning impact for his or her students. Students can interact in ways that he or she could not in a more traditional learning environment, perform tasks that they normally could not, and/or build curiosity for future learning or apply face-to-face learning.

In conclusion, flipping the classroom really forces teachers to have a deeper understanding and appreciation of instructional time and how to maximize it both online and face-to-face. Flipping the classroom allows the teacher to perform tasks online that could be considered a waste of face-to-face time. Face-to-face time, regardless of meeting schedule, becomes more invaluable and should not be wasted. Finally, the flipped environment allows for the taking of more risks. The online environment allows teachers to attempt activities that they might not otherwise create for their students. If the activities are successful, they can be repeated and possibly even expanded on a larger scale in either a face-to-face or an online environment. If they do not work, minimal damage has been done. In other words, there will be some flops when flipping the classroom. The key for both students and teachers is to be flexible and admit mistakes. When flipping the classroom, especially until the environment has been established institution-wide, students and teachers are in the experiment together. How rich of a learning experience can it be when both students and teachers can not only learn together but also from one another? Flipping the classroom, like any other instructional tool, should be used in the best manner possible. Even (and maybe especially) on a small scale, flipping the classroom can be highly successful and valuable.

"If you want transformational change,
roll up your sleeves and get ready to do some heavy lifting."

-Dr. John Ross

Chapter 9

Tech-tonic Shifts

Getting yourself aboard the technology train is one thing; setting your intentions toward a whole school or an entire district is quite another. This is, however, the dilemma with which our nation's educational systems are faced. When our district decided to make this monumental shift, we hired an expert by the name of Dr. John Ross. A delightful man, Ross, who is a teacher, writer, and well-known tech consultant, guided our administrators and the 21st Century pilot teachers on our journey toward infusing technology and digital literacy into our curricula. I could think of no better person to lend advice about the big picture.

Tech-tonic Shifts
John D. Ross

I'm not sure whether she realized it or not, but Susan has selected an ironically appropriate topic *and* title for my contribution. As a former music teacher, I'm pretty well versed in the idea of tonics as they relate to sound. That combined with my current status of helping educators plan for, integrate, and evaluate technology-based initiatives can truly be summed up as approaching the idea of "tech-tonic" shifts from many perspectives. In music, tonic shifts (some might say modulations) follow certain rules or guidelines. They are usually prepared for, some quite eloquently so. Sure, some day an Arnold Schoenberg will come along and bend those rules completely, but, in all reality, he and his contemporaries were also working from some very strict rules of their own. Every domain has some accepted ways of doing things, and we can all learn by knowing some of those rules or guidelines.

Unlike musical composition, there may not be hard-and-fast "rules" for technology integration (or any other change effort), but there are certainly lessons learned—both in education and from the larger field of organizational change. After leaving the classroom, a fortuitous accident led me to further study in instructional design for both general education and corporate training. Adventures in this field include product and program evaluation as well as providing technical assistance to a wide range of folks. Some of this has been official, such as serving in leadership roles for a Regional Education

Laboratory and two Comprehensive Centers, both of which are programs funded by the U.S. Department of Education. The latter, the Comprehensive Center, is specifically charged with "building the capacity" of state education agencies, a daunting task, if you think about it. And not one to take lightly. Show up on the front step of any SEA and say, "I'm here to build your capacity," and you won't make it past the door.

So, with a few well-earned battle scars and even a few checkmarks in the win column, with those in the other column probably providing stronger evidence for what *not* to do, I hope to share a few ideas. I've culled these from my experiences from working with educators from across the country in terms of supporting organizational change—from single schools to entire states. Whether wanting to focus on isolated integration in a single classroom or school or working on whole-scale organizational change, these are some of the rules I've learned.

I. Continuum Theory

While I often work with schools and districts that are beginning their journey of technology integration, we've been using digital technologies in classrooms for quite some time. While I didn't use a personal computer in my own education until working on my Master's degree, computers have been in classrooms for almost half a century! That means lots of years of experiences and lessons learned. One of the most important lessons learned that I keep returning to time and time again is one that comes from those early days of integration, and that is, as teachers (and school leaders) integrate technology, they do so across a continuum. This lesson was first (and perhaps best) presented by researchers for the Apple Classrooms of Tomorrow (ACOT) project in the 1980s (Dwyer, Ringstaff, & Sandholtz, 1991). Yes, the 1980s. We've been doing this "tech stuff" that long.

The basic lesson from that time is that not all educators adopt technology to the same degree at the same time, but most more or less follow a continuum of adoption that they join at different points. Well, we hope they all move up the continuum. Some do. Some we need to keep working on. I've found this continuum theory holds true in every technology initiative I've worked with. It's also mentioned repeatedly in the literature since the 80s in various reincarnations, such as the National Educational Technology Standards for Teachers (NETS-T) from ISTE (see http://www.iste.org/standards/standards-for-teachers) and the (what's old is new again) SAMR model. Maybe *I* need to recycle some decades old idea with a new label?

The ACOT researchers described their continuum with 5 stages, from Entry to Innovation. Along the way, teachers build their skills and knowledge and learn how technology provides support to create learning opportunities that just can't be done without the technology. Yes, I went there. Things you *can't do* without technology. It's not just about efficiency. It's about creating new learning environments. Need proof?

In Virginia, students can access and control the same telescopes astronomers and other space scientists do to explore the night sky (the catch is the Virginia telescope is in Australia because it's night there when our kids are in school). There are other probes students can interact with, from the bottom of the Puget Sound to a rover on Mars. Students are also interacting with their favorite authors and others through telecommunications that bring them into their classrooms in real time or through asynchronous blogs or chats. And kids are running their own businesses, filming their own documentaries, and writing their own apps. Do that with paper and pencil.

It takes some time to get to that stage, however, whether you think of the continuum as having 3, 4, or 5 stages. ACOT says 5. ISTE says 4. I sum it up in 3:

> 1. **Replication.** Teachers begin by using technology to replicate what they are familiar with. If they are familiar with a lecture followed by student handouts, they might support a lecture with presentation software and print out (or post digital) handouts for students to complete. If they like collaborative groups and problem-based learning, they incorporate technologies that allow students to work together in and outside of the classroom and solve problems.
>
> 2. **Adoption.** Teachers start to see the value of technology, become more efficient at what they do, and even try some new things that the technology makes easier or more effective. Gradebooks and lesson planning tools are ones that many teachers first see

increased benefit from using. Not only do they make grading easier and save time in terms of creating, storing, and sharing lessons, but these tools also have added benefits like securely sharing grades with students, sending out notifications, running reports, and even providing communication opportunities with parents.

3. **Transformation.** This is where teachers create activities or entire learning environments that just can't be done without the technology. I've given some examples, but what might be considered transformative is continuing to change. We've seen this recently with the widespread emphasis of personalized learning, blended learning, mobile learning, competency-based learning and the impact these trends are having on well-worn (and some would say outdated) educational stalwarts, such as seat-time and Carnegie units.

All of this may be interesting, but what does this mean for supporting change? How does this promote technology integration? For me, the **golden rule** of the continuum is: *you have to meet the teacher where s/he is.* A teacher at any stage can use technology effectively and promote student learning. If the teacher is at the replicate stage, a change agent (often a technology coach) can focus efforts on supporting teachers as they learn to use technology to replicate what they feel comfortable with. When they're ready to move, they will, if given the support they need. Transformation, while fun, can also be challenging. And if you're not there, don't expect to get there immediately. Maybe not even in a year. And some teachers just might not get there.

My hope is that all teachers first feel comfortable in the stage they naturally find themselves and occasionally push themselves beyond. Those who may not believe transformation is their goal might benefit from working with someone who is in that stage because it is possible for all teachers. But it doesn't have to happen every day or every lesson. The first goal for all teachers is promoting student learning, and change agents can help teachers reach this goal every stage of the continuum.

II. What type of change do you want?

I have the great privilege of working with one of my professional mentors. Dr. Sharon Harsh is an exemplary educator who is also an acknowledged national leader in the field of organizational change, especially as it relates to education. She has studied the organizational change literature across many industries and has used that knowledge to craft strategies and procedures to support systemic change at the statewide level to much success. For this, she is acknowledged by the U.S. Department of Education, and I get to pick her brain often and learn from her. How cool is that?

Early in the change process, those in charge really should sit down and determine what kind of change they're really seeking. Harsh (2012) summarizes that there are three levels of change and that using strategies for one type to address another not only can be ineffective but also can frustrate those involved and hamper the ability to implement future change initiatives. She describes three types of change:

1. **Incremental** or **first-order change** occurs when a change initiative is localized to an individual or small group of individuals within an organization. In schools, this can occur when a group of teachers takes a class or attends a training together in order to implement a strategy they've learned. Or perhaps a grade-level team may work on adopting a new technology resource together. In this type of change, an individual may build capacity, but the organization as a whole stays very much the same.

2. **Transitional** or **second-order change** ramps things up a bit. This type of change focuses at a larger group of people, a well-defined group, such as a workgroup or a team in an organization. In schools, this could be a group like all counselors, all algebra teachers, or all technology

coaches (to use a Dubuque example). The goal of second-order change is to help an entire subgroup of the organization build their capacity to meet the goals of the organization, but whole-scale organizational change is still not occurring.

3. **Transformational** change or **third-order change** is true systemic change in which all of the players in an organization are impacted, some profoundly. This type of change is, obviously, the most challenging type of change to undergo and see to a successful conclusion because it can impact the entire culture of the organization. It may require people to reflect and modify their philosophy of their role in the organization and what they want to get out of being in the organization. Some may leave the organization. In a successful transformational change, everyone changes to some degree.

Again, more great lessons, but what does this mean for schools? Especially those in the midst of a tech-tonic shift? In my experience, the most obvious answer rests in the mismatch between intentions of a change initiative and the strategies used to get there. Transformational change is hard. It's complex and requires a great deal of preparation and forethought. As Harsh is fond of quoting, "Complex problems require complex solutions." Simplistic approaches won't lead to successful change in complex situations, like whole-organization change. Transformational change is truly a contact sport. It requires rallying the troops and getting everyone on the same page. It can even involve thinning the troops or finding those more simpatico to the change vision.

In my experience, too many education organizations attempt to implement transformational change through incremental strategies—using simplistic strategies that can't address a complex problem. In most cases, those I work with are seeking transformational change whether they originally intend to or not. Also, in most of these cases, the strategies used are limited to individuals or a small group or do not tackle the larger and more complex issues related to revising personal philosophies, developing a shared vision, or changing organizational culture. Yes, those are challenging aspects, which may be why so many people want to avoid them, but you have to be true to yourselves and those with whom you work. If you want transformational change, roll up your sleeves and get ready to do some heavy lifting. If you're not ready for the long-term investment required for transformational change, change your sights. Focus on incremental change and select strategies that will support it.

III. Basic needs of capacity-building

In 2013, I helped the Appalachia Regional Comprehensive Center (ARCC, 2013) put together a two-day regional seminar on systemic change. Presenters came from several states along with the U.S. Department of Education and the Council of Chief State School Officers. At the opening session, Eric Oetjen, a senior vice president for ICF International, the organization that holds the ARCC contract, opened the seminar with a few experiences from his own work supporting large-scale, capacity-building efforts, especially in areas related to social change.

Eric eloquently and quickly laid the groundwork for the seminar by outlining four key components that anyone implementing a capacity building change effort should consider. (He was so good that he was later featured in a one-hour webinar in which he was given more time to expand on these ideas. You can find the webinar archive at arccta.org.) Eric gave these four guidelines that I believe represent some key basic needs for supporting capacity building change. I elaborate on each briefly in relation to technology initiatives, specifically, which is where I most often see these coming into play.

1. **Think broadly about the stakeholders and engage them early.** Too often technology initiatives are seen as external to the day-to-day work of the school, which is promoting student learning. Technology initiatives are often isolated, sometimes stigmatized, so it's difficult to get widespread buy-in. Sometimes we think it's only the IT staff or the technology coach that needs to buy-in, but any successful school initiative will include all stakeholders, from administrators, teachers, and other staff to parents and—most importantly—the students. Eric notes that if you don't engage all stakeholders early, you're going to have to at some point in order to be successful. I add that if you don't plan to engage them

early, you may not like how some of them get involved and the negative impact some stakeholders can have on even the most worthwhile initiative.

2. **Move towards a common language.** I sometimes think that educators are the worst in terms of jargon—what I call "educationese." I'm sure every industry has its own, but in education, we use so many common words (e.g., authentic, engaged, problem, project, assessment) that often end up meaning very different things in an educational setting. Eric warns that if change leaders don't help everyone come to a common understanding of key terms, concepts, and process, people end up "talking past each other." Common language, of course, starts with a clear vision and constantly referring to that vision to make sure your initiative is on track. But I've gone so far as to creating "word walls" or glossaries of key terms to help everyone get on the same page.

3. **Develop a communication strategy.** Eric suggests having a clear communication strategy that is implemented early and regularly can make or break a change effort. This really can't be underemphasized. When I work with organizations and ask about communication, it's often sloughed off as if "been there, done that." People will cite organizational newsletters, websites, meetings, without ever determining if anyone

actually reads or pays attention to these things. Don't take communication for granted. I led a team of about two dozen educators through an audit-type visit of a large school district in my state. The superintendent told me we should look for innovative use of technology which he had been pushing for innovation since he got there. What we found was that communication—from the central office to the schools to the classrooms and back up that chain—was lacking. Remedying this was the top priority we encouraged the superintendent to consider in order to reach his goals. It turned out no one had the same idea of what innovation was, and so any use of technology, from using an overhead projector on up, ended up being considered innovative. Not exactly what the superintendent had in mind.

4. **Design for early results.** This was a unique suggestion Eric made, that I would not have included, but it makes perfect sense upon reflection. As an instructional designer, I incorporate strategies to motivate the learner based on the work of John Keller who developed the ARCS motivational design model (A = get the learners Attention, R = make the material Relevant, C = build the learner's Confidence, S = ensure the learner is Successful.) I use this model often and try to be sure that the materials I develop allow the learner to be successful early. Start with small success to build

motivation and increase complexity over time. Eric suggested a similar philosophy, noting that even if you can accomplish small or even temporary results early, they will build momentum for the initiative and help it keep moving forward. Same idea. I'm glad he applied it to capacity building.

Learning from Los Angeles

Unfortunately, the Los Angeles Unified School District suffered through one of the least successful technology integration efforts perhaps in the history of schools—at least since personal computers were introduced into schools in the 80s. Costing more than a billion dollars and a much reported dismal failure—one that cost the superintendent his job—the one good thing that came out of the effort are some lessons learned. These five lessons were posted in *Edutopia* (Gliksman, 2014) and should serve as the basis for anyone planning any technology initiative in the future.

1. Change starts with a vision.
2. Top-down strategies rarely work without communication and consensus.
3. Training requires more than an introductory "how-to" workshop.
4. Technology should empower students.
5. It's not about the device.

IV. What can schools do to support change?

So, now you've gotten started. You've bought some new materials, perhaps some technology devices or new curricular materials, or you've brought in some trainer to help spread the word. Boxes have been opened, people have been trained...now what? Unfortunately, this is when a lot of initiatives fall short. They're front-loaded with planning and training, but the resources aren't put into place to nurture and sustain the effort. I can tell when I visit a school or district with a follow through problem when teachers (or other staff) talk about "what we did last year," or even the year before and there's no clear connection from year to year or initiative to initiative.

This also happens in those districts or schools with implementation overload. Every year someone introduces new materials, new methods, new devices with no clear long-range plan that ties them all together. I was visiting one school where the faculty complained they had "too much" training. They were introduced to so many things, they said it was like a buffet. But in the end, as one overwhelmed teacher told me, "Just show me 1 or 2 things that work and give me time to really learn how to use it."

I developed the following guidance for school leaders implementing technology initiatives in their schools, but they could help anyone charged with implementing change. You'll see some advice repeated from earlier, but that just highlights the importance of some of these strategies. This list began with advice from Margaret Heritage (2010), but I've combined some items and school it down to be a little more manageable.

1. **Communicate.** This bears repeating. School leaders articulate, and constantly communicate, the value of any

change effort. This begins with and returns to the vision, but it has to be relevant. If it's not important to school leadership, it's not important to teachers. Administrators who don't buy in to a change effort can actually derail it. School leaders help everyone—teachers, other staff, parents, students—understand the importance of the initiative and reinforce it through multiple and varied communications.

2. **Support.** School leaders provide *explicit* support to their teachers and staff related to the effort. People participating in and impacted by the change will need different kinds of support. Often, this implies new kinds of support. Determine what kind of support is needed. Be specific. Avoid platitudes or overgeneralizing. Yes, teachers need professional development, but what kind? Lesson study, observations, time to collaborate? Yes, people will need time, but what kind of time specifically? Time to collaborate, to plan, to experiment? Identify the types of support and prioritize those needs.

3. **Dedicate time:** School leaders find and *protect* time to engage in real work around the change initiative. Change efforts require ongoing time for meeting, reflection, and discussion. If these times succumb to other meetings or duties, the change won't occur. Many schools have professional learning communities (PLCs), some just in name only. Any change effort, if worth

doing, should be incorporated into existing PLC efforts. Every PLC meeting should result in some tangible outcome related to the change effort.

4. **Embed and connect:** School leaders make connections to other initiatives. Teachers don't have a lot of time, so even the best intended initiative won't be effective if they don't understand how new initiatives support existing initiatives or processes. School leaders should make these connections explicit, communicate them often, and tie them together. If a new technology initiative is implemented, school leaders help teachers understand how it will impact or support lesson planning, instruction, classroom observations, communications with students and parents—everything.

5. **Allocate resources:** School leaders make strategic decisions about the allocation of resources that support the initiative. Not all resources require new funding. New initiatives should be implemented as an effort to address an existing need. Is literacy an issue? How will the change initiative support literacy? Conduct an analysis of what does and doesn't work and get rid of those that don't! Too many schools hand on to legacy programs that are ineffective just because "that's the way we do it around here." It can also help to get staff from different departments, along with the budgets they oversee, to get together and see how a new effort can

support their work. Very often, technology initiatives can support multiple programs (e.g., title programs, special education, literacy, and technology programs) and can be made affordable when budgets are combined across programs, something that may not be attainable by a single program's budget.

6. **Take risks:** School leaders establish and nurture an atmosphere of risk taking and learning from mistakes. School leaders will have to consider how they deal with taking risks and making mistakes. Teachers are not the only ones who will be trying new things or having to learn new skills. School leaders should be sure to learn alongside teachers by determining which trainings and meetings they'll participate in with teachers. They may also want to consider which meetings they *won't* participate in, in case teachers want some time to practice and work on their own.

7. **Acknowledge and celebrate!** School leaders comment on, encourage, and celebrate teachers who demonstrate positive aspects of the initiative. Whenever a school leader visits a classroom, they should be sure to recognize aspects of the initiative (catch teachers doing good things drawn from the initiative) and comment on and encourage teachers who are doing so. And plan for and implement celebration! What celebrations are already in place where teachers and others can be

acknowledged for the work they're doing? Can they be acknowledged at staff meetings, daily announcements, with letters or cards, in newsletters, or on digital media like the school website, Facebook page, or other means? Celebration is fun and encouraging but often overlooked.

I encourage school or change leaders to do an analysis of existing strategies and processes that support each of these seven strategies. Include people responsible for them, such as the school secretary that puts together the school newsletter where you're going to acknowledge the good work of your teachers or the department heads that are going to carry your message back to their colleagues on a daily basis. Determine what works and whom to involve.

You may also need to develop or implement new strategies. For example, some schools may have department meetings but not really PLCs. If you plan to support the change effort with teachers from multiple departments, schools may need to find and adopt a PLC model to help organize those meetings and make them more effective.

In summary, I suggest that we, as an education community, know a lot about implementing and sustaining successful change initiatives. Unfortunately, we, as individual educators, may not always know about this body of knowledge nor about the strategies necessary to successfully implement change. Hopefully this brief overview provides some concrete ideas and strategies for those either leading or succumbing to change efforts and will find it helpful to make those change efforts more successful.

References

ARCC. (July 18-19, 2013). *Exploring the parameters of systemic change and capacity.* Regional Systemic Capacity Seminar, Crystal City, VA.

Dwyer, D. C, Ringstaff, C, & Sandholtz, J. H. (1991). Changes in teachers' beliefs and practices in technology-rich classrooms. *Educational Leadership, 48* (8), 45-52.

Gliksman, S. (2014). The LAUSD iPad initiative: 5 critical technology integration lessons. *Edutopia.* Available from: http://www.edutopia.org/blog/lausd-ipad-technology-integration-lessons-sam-gliksman

Harsh, S. (2012). *Taking successful change initiatives beyond capacity: multiple-dimension approach to capacity building.* Fairfax, VA: ICF International.

Heritage, M. (2010). *Formative assessment. Making it happen in the classroom.* Thousand Oaks, CA: Corwin.

Keller, J. M. (1987). Strategies for stimulating the motivation to learn. *Performance and Instruction, 26*(8), 1-7.

Keep the kids your priority…

Chapter 10
Get Tech

This is the first time I have written a book. It took me several years to manage it because the publishing realm seemed daunting. To finish the text would mean I would be compelled to immerse myself in a world with which I was unfamiliar. I was afraid of this uncertain and foreign territory. Nonetheless, I said to myself: swifty, 'tis time. Do what your book suggests. Dive in. Finish the text and find out what you need to do to publish.

I sought some advice from colleagues who had published, and I read online advice from experts in the field. I investigated copyrights, ISBNs, and royalties. It was a steep learning curve but not an insurmountable one.

I decided to self-publish and, with that, I was beset multiple issues as I attempted to set up the pagination. I texted my tech consultant and, with plenty of expletives, described my utter frustration with technology. The Word program I was using was completely uncooperative as I tried to insert Roman page numbers in the initial pages and Arabic ones for the text. I took my own advice and looked at YouTube videos and tossed my questions into Google. I learned about section breaks, followed the directions precisely, and, alas, I still could not get it to work. At long last, I bailed and uploaded this document into a brand-new template and wrestled with both the technology and my shortcomings until it worked. Upon finally figuring it out, I shared the celebratory news with my tech consultant, to which he quipped, "Think of how this part of your story will be a great closure to your book."

My response: "Ugh."

Life sometimes seems like a series of ironies, does it not? Here I am, trying to encourage others to take the tech challenges in stride, while at the same time, I am tempted to pitch my new computer like frisbee into a heavily trafficked street.

But, as I mentioned in the prologue, what we want to do and what we should do are often in conflict, and we must lean toward our higher, more rational purpose. And ours is to better educate our students.

Begin by reframing your existence from "I'm behind" to "I am going to try something technologically innovative to help my students more readily learn." Then, dive in. Unabashedly.

Unapologetically. Do something. *Anything.* Compare your current challenge to physical exercise—it doesn't really matter what you do to get yourself in better shape; it only matters that you move. So, move. Accept the inevitable learning curve and the necessary collaborative nature of learning to effectively use technology. "The sage on the stage" is, for all practical purposes, over. (Thankfully.) Remember, only a temporary state is "iDumb"—that is until you hit your next great classroom idea! Choose an educational lens that works best for you and your students and put that pair of specs on each time you plan. Let go of the buzz, the lingo, the jargon, the acronymic language, and catch phrases. Instead, speak with your unique, needful voice. Think about your summative assessments as you re-envision the work you do for your students. From there, choose tech tools that will increase learning and engagement. Be not afraid to reinvent your classroom with practices you never before imagined. It is exhilarating. Consider joining the bigger picture by volunteering to be on school- and/or district-wide committees whose purpose is to effectively deepen critical digital literacy and inventive learning for all students—and for all teachers. Keep the kids your priority and invite them to help you design your newly unfolding pedagogy. Now go. Get tech!

References

Bertolucci, J. (2012, May 09). Angry birds reaches 1
   billion downloads. Retrieved from https://www.pcworld.co
   m/article/255337/angry_birds_reaches_ 1_billion_downloa
   ds.html

Burke, J. (2010). *What's the big idea?: Question-driven
   units to motivate reading, writing and thinking.*
   Portsmouth, NH: Heinemann.

Chappuis, J. (2015). *Seven strategies of assessment for
   learning.* Boston: Pearson.

Commiserate - Dictionary Definition. (n.d.). Retrieved
   from https://www.vocabulary.com/dictionary/commiserate

Iowa CORE. (n.d.). Retrieved from
   https://iowacore.gov/iowa-core/subject/literacy

Kendall, P. (2011, February 07). Angry birds, the story
   behind iPhone's gaming phenomenon. Retrieved from
   https://www.telegraph.co.uk/technology/video-
   games/8303173/Angry-Birds-the-story-behind-iPhones-
   gaming-phenomenon.html

Know the ISTE Standards for Students 1. (n.d.).
   Retrieved from
   https://www.iste.org/explore/ISTE-Standards-in-
   Action/Know-the-ISTE-Standards-for-Students-1

Know the ISTE Standards for Students, Standard 2:
   Communication and Collaboration. (n.d.).
   Retrieved from

https://www.iste.org/explore/ISTE-Standards-in-
Action/Know-the-ISTE-Standards-for-Students,-Standard-
2:-Communication-and-Collaboration

Manafy, M. (2009, February 18). Alacra puts its finger
on the pulse of business information. Retrieved from
http://www.econtentmag.com/Articles/ News/News-
Feature/Alacra-Puts-its-Finger-on-the-Pulse-of-Business-
Information-52670.htm.

Rubenking, N. J. (2018, January 25). LastPass.
Retrieved from
https://www.pcmag.com/review/317662/lastpas

Rubenking, N. J. (2019, May 01). The best password
managers for 2019.   Retrieved from
https://www.pcmag.com/roundup/300318/the-best-
password-managers

Search Engine Market Share Worldwide. (n.d.).
Retrieved from
http://gs.statcounter.com/search-engine-market-
share

Ultra VNC remote access tools. (n.d.). Retrieved from
https://www.uvnc.com/

Why use Symbaloo? (n.d.). Retrieved from
https://en.help.symbaloo.com/portal/kb/articles/why-use-
symbaloo- 22-2-2018

ABOUT THE AUTHOR

Susan Swift taught in secondary schools for thirty-five years. Since retiring from this work, she has been active writing, teaching yoga, and supervising student teachers for Loras College and the University of Dubuque. Swift is a published poet, essayist, and lyricist. She resides in Dubuque, Iowa.

Made in the USA
Monee, IL
18 May 2020

31427225R00066